The Oratory of All Souls

Also by Richard Robbins:

POETRY:

Other Americas

Radioactive City

The Untested Hand

Famous Persons We Have Known

The Invisible Wedding

Body Turn to Rain: New & Selected Poems

CHAPBOOKS:

Toward New Weather

ANTHOLOGIES:

Where We Are: The Montana Poets Anthology
(with co-editor Lex Runciman)

The Oratory of All Souls

Richard Robbins

Lynx House Press

SPOKANE, WASHINGTON

Printed in the United States of America

Published by Lynx House Press, Spokane, Washington

Cover art *Memory of Water: Shoreline* by Brian Frink, Watercolor, 2014
Used by permission
Author photo credit: Minnesota State Mankato
Interior and cover design by Jodi Miller-Hunter

FIRST EDITION

Cataloging-in-Publication Data is available from the Library of Congress

ISBN 978-0-89924-190-6

For my lost sister and brother

CONTENTS

2. DISAPPEARANCES

3. THE ORATORY OF ALL SOULS

4. THAT BEACH

WAVE

Every day and always, the stray pebble finds him, an eye looking up from the
path to another's execution, the camouflaged jury of peers, beneath which
the earth goes on with its thinking.

How will he ever know the way around it, eye looking out from a 900-year-old
painting on granite, eye of salmon up from the depths of a glacial lake, eye of
octopus and rat, eye of daisy, eye at the end of a sentence.

On long drives across desert, the earth has its way with him, wind and grit in
his face, his neck turned to leather. The sun screams quietly. The large birds
circle.

Over the mountains, he smells the ocean salt again, the smell of a son's head
moments after birth. The basin spreads out 80 miles toward the sea, basin
of a million homes, a hundred thousand crimes of love or theft, acts of
mercy one at a time under a fog that will leave God blind for hours. Cars
explode across the arteries expanding in every direction. The salt settles on
everything, living or dead.

Every day and always, the wave that spins above him, a bright wash of
turbulence, a prayer for the new life. He lets tide pull him from the sandy
shore. He walks avenues of the great western city, nodding to strangers,
casual with air, even as the undertow nags at his feet, even as persons on the
beach will blur into the white of their own care.

How will he ever know the daily way back to solid ground, to loved ones with
their own rituals of renewal.

How will he know the eye falls beyond him. Even the machinery of the world
will find its way back from loss. Even as it carries the grief of billions. Even
as the blood on its surface, blood of birth or blood of revolution, raises the
flag of its shame and its reward.

1

1. The Blue Houses

All's a scattering,
A shining.

—Theodore Roethke

AT THE SHORE

I begin with the soul, that escape
artist, that meme. And what the dress draped
across the beach chair will shout like a clue
to each wave. And what bodies will make

of disappearance. And what, since I
have begun, the abandoned body
gathers to its tote now along with towel,
snacks, and creams. And what sunlight reading

comes home to a dark house. And what new
absence a mortal discovers. You
couldn't know what happens, the emptiness
says. Even the dust has moved away.

SURFACING

All his friends damaged into poems
want to know where that leaves him, what

dark heart preyed upon his, what early
death reset the poles for the long

earthwalk through words to now. They
couldn't know the first trout, sidling

on the bank, the air creosote
and thin at that altitude, or

the water all night creekside, free
with its secret—what we call joy.

Or they can't remember the rise,
the swimming sideways or down but

rising anyway, pulled gingerly
on a line, a kind of violence,

a death to quiet, and the old
eyes that couldn't see yet, God

help him, and no new way to breathe,
but the light. But the light.

BEGIN

Halfway to zero, the heart began to count its beats. A thumb knuckle made of itself
the hinge between two worlds.

At 8000 feet in the middle of Sweetwater Creek, brown trout swam around his legs
in the shimmering light beneath aspens. The air thickened with lint and the
frenzied death of insects.

Once again he found himself at the center of two great sufferings.

Once again the line unraveling west for 1200 miles, to unspoken savagery at
the shore. The line a muscle made across template of bone. A road. The line
unraveling, canyon by canyon, episode by episode, through time.

Once again the wreckage he passed just getting to the edge of this wilderness. The tin
hut glaring. The tin hut glaring.

Halfway to zero, the mind had wanted to play along. He was only half responsible
for the burning mountain sun. Half of his grief lay behind him, in the yellow
waterproof bag.

If trout struck his fly, another world would be calling. Halfway through his life, he
wouldn't know how to answer. Miles away, the mouths of those children kept
tugging at their hooks. By that hour, a few cars would be going up and through
the final layer of summit, through the 10-mile tunnel to a place where the other
big river would begin.

SOMEONE ELSE'S MAP

Who would put the first bird, a Stellar's jay, on their map. Or the first fern,
   swiveling now on its stalk not in wind but in a wave of heat rising from the
   spot where first sun fell across the frost.
Who would absolve the first offender, no matter her non-intent, no matter any
   later generosity.
Listen: When someone draws the map of his grief, he includes white spaces that
   are never only loss. A herd of elk passes through this part of the woods every
   night, never detected. They are crossing the white space now.
Listen: You have to roll your own grief inside the leather bundle and stow it
   on the mud porch. It will stay warm there, even though you may want it
   outdoors hanging in the light and cold air. You have to count everything
   inside the bundle and leave it right there on the wooden slats, next to the
   shoes. It made you afraid once, to walk away.
Who would leave his house and walk the thin highway a mile north to that
   village. Who would stop at every front gate blessing it, even if the house had
   been empty for years, the family all dead, its fortune played out, even if it's
   only a set for some historical reenactment.
Who would leave himself behind.
Even though that, all along, made the color for the map, the direction of its
   rivers, configured it, as in ancient times, with south at the top—that place of
   community and good weather. Who would cross the white behind the first
   things of this world only to discover weightlessness and the light of animals.
   Question after question a string of tracks in the dark across windfall and duff.

LEADBETTER POINT

Salal along the trail from Leadbetter Point
down to the Bay. Goat's beard lichen on every
kind of tree. The Sitka spruce. The elkhorn
moss. The broken empty egg of plover.
The washed-up, upturned crab. The vegetable
scat of coyote. The elk, ghosts of the forest,
moving bayside to oceanside and back
and no one knowing. The sun rising
from behind the coast range, rising across
the clam and oyster water. And ocean
wind subsumed by fir and cedar in the mile
between there and here. And shade settling onto the grove
of old growth. You are never really
alone. Not with your lost sister's face
still in the chop. Your grandfather's voice drifting
up the tidal flat from a cluster
of boats. Not with your wife and sons still moving
slowly in Midwest ice far over
those mountains like a dream. The mind
could sweep them away, or the mind
could fail, and still the inner weather would find
these monochrome grasses more beautiful
than color. This clump of ditch weed tamped down
by bears. The bald eagle screech sudden
and invisible. The heartbreak moment
to moment, run through by swords, because break
and mend is everything you didn't
know you missed. Or so the angel will tell you
once you recover again, or stand
upright again, once you move your mouth
around the holy host of first words.

SECRET FATHER, BEGINNINGS

What would it mean they knew him father
all along, holding a finger, then
the whole hand, kissing him good night, before
each year the steady, cold erasure,

first the two arms meant to hold them, ears
intent to hear. Science or magic,
he could barely find himself those mornings
discovering the closet empty,

half his body become the space he
used to fill, all his voice the silence
they had groomed him to enter, dividing
even, finally, from each other, three

hearts now, three bodies disappearing
into separate slipstreams, three hearts left
to name each invisible self, the air
and landscape of each quiet continent.

MY FATHER DOES NOT REVEAL HIMSELF

Or he hears us calling and doesn't know
how to answer with what a father's belt
could do when he was eight, or what it was

about our mother he can still remember
loving. We can sit these long hot backyard
afternoons of dog and ball, and still

the sky's too thin to hang a story on.
What makes him joyful now? If not his dad,
who taught him how to be a man? His new captors

ask these questions, these children he barely
knows, those convinced language is the drug
if not the cure. We talk to the one who

couldn't find the phrase to say their grandmother
died until weeks later. Who knows a word
keeps a beating alive, and all grief close

at hand. Better to be ninety, off-balance,
a little deaf, even though these last
loved ones will not cross into that silence.

MEMORY OF WATER / ISLAND

—a painting by Brian Frink, 2014

Day and night we stopped what we were doing
to find ourselves swimming toward it. It was
God, it was the other we'd have to cross

the great deep to love.
We memorized its jagged back in the bottomless
hour of night. Beyond that spine of tree crown and rock

lay the line of a far-off range. Beyond that,
the unhinging of stars.
We heard its voice after a while—not God's, not

the other's—something any wind might say
to a fox. It starts each morning with the surface chop,
the same wind talking to blue.

Year by year, these same red nets of routine. What
happens to a city if we leave it? How does
the wild place die in our hands? We ask you,

great one, O lover. We are swimming
over parables of weed and bass, under
the unstoried sky of day. We will praise you, moving

in your direction. We will praise you closing
in on us, even in your delay.

LOOKING FOR THE MAN IN A FIELD

Would the man stand at the end of a knife, the turned-up head of cauliflower.

Would the man wipe sweat from his face, fold a red handkerchief for his pocket.

Would he sit in the dust and shade beside his truck and laugh between bites of a sandwich.

Would he whistle as long as the tractor starts.

Would the man say a rosary for each row of grapes or lettuce.

Would the man curse or befriend the sun.

Would he become the movement of an arm, a leg.

Would he think himself some other place, on a front walk where Marisol, Peter, where even Hector the good dog would greet him after the light had failed.

Would the man burn to nothing like morning fog in the rows.

Would the man leave his shadow there.

Would he walk back out of darkness like a ghost or like dawn.

Would any word he is saying come from the dark, the light, or the vine.

Did it find the man in the field.

Did he and the field move inside each other until the word found his tongue.

AT SPIRAL JETTY

Secret Father's city reeks of salt,
its passengers on ghost trains rolling over each Chinese bone.

He sent you a mother-song from Kansas.
He sent you a salmon run.

Black stone turns into itself on the sand.
Secret Father would reveal himself at the shore, but all the scud delivers is
     magnesium.

He sends you ashes from Kansas.
He sends you a salmon run.

Blue-green lake breathes in and out from its edge.
The delivery was scheduled for this moment

but mountains veer away on each horizon:
You're nowhere to be found.

LOOKING FOR THE MAN IN A DRIVEWAY

We stood around, looked in different
directions, and one of us said
the sky resembled the sky,
years ago, he had camped beneath,

firs bent in a gale. Cars went by,
and we analyzed their color
or trim, if they were crap cars
or decent, and eventually

we talked about women, or tried,
but we'd been married so long we'd
forgotten the old language,
how even to remember what

men don't speak about anyway,
how the smell of her hair warmed him,
how in the tent she undressed
in the dark to hide her freckled

shoulders, how he kissed each one, that
skin, the sunburn, the pale country
halter top and shorts had saved
all day hiking to the glacier.

SECRET FATHER, TABLES TURNED

That day at the reading of the will,
each surprising property was named
by township and lot, the disposition
of an antique chair, ten culled shotguns

for grandchildren, an Asian rug. His
sister, he learns, is his mother, sky
suddenly entering the board room where
the lawyer keeps reading sentences

about the year he was born, the small
minds in those parts, the letter lying
on the wood grain as the eyes, not his, search
for him in the glare. His sister is

his mother, and his father: likely
the one he thought his uncle, the one
who always limped like he does now, at home
in the field retrieving downed birds, in

how he complimented the sister's
hair, her dress, all those things an uncle
or lover would do. In the bright of room,
the sky widens. The family, facing

more business, wants to move on,
and he no longer sure of his name.

THE COUNTY PARK IN FALL

Secret Father envied the men at cross country meets, weighed down with
    cameras and swagger, those who could buy a child's love one milkshake, one
    set of racing spikes at a time.
From the small hill he watched the junior and senior boys and girls, four races,
    making their separate loops through open green and trails, singlets flicking
    between each tree until runners emerged for a last dash to the finish.
The fathers waited beside the narrowing chute, nailed shoulder to shoulder to
    those like them. In the dark of their pockets, each flicked a stopwatch off. In
    the dark of winter, they would plot the times on a graph.
Secret Father walked among them after the last race. Everyone's breath had
    begun to cloud.
He would make plans throughout winter, lines in a book about how to draw
    them closer together, even as they pushed each other apart.
It was hard work, not fully understanding human beings but, like an angel,
    needing to watch over them.
Secret Father understood his vocation, if never fully the tool or the way.

DOCUMENTARY

In the bermed hut I lived in for a month,
a peat fire constant in the hearth,
I made the tea and roasted lamb and read,
barely wondering about the man

who lived there too, naked as I, shaved
head to foot, sleeping when I awoke,
awake when I slept, and for a few hours
each day, the one I stepped around, quiet,

the same for both of us, our habits
someone else's art. We ate and shat
and dreamed wet dreams and read about the war
and wrote letters home, never knowing

how a camera caught us, where on earth
we were. Then the door opened to hills
grassy and endless. Then the two of us
embracing. He heading south and down

to tumbled water, I to the hilltop,
where the wind blew fierce, and clouds scudded
toward city or ocean—they didn't care—
the hilltop where the chimney of our hut

squatted like a cairn venting its smoke,
where I could look into it and down
and see beyond the glow of earth burning
two men still there, never speaking,

going about their business under ground.

SECRET FATHER ROLLOVER

In the white skid on black ice,
in the ditch between the legs,

he would assemble the son part by part if there were time,
each finger a bass line, each toe the note of a flute.

The radio would warn of weather.
There would be lanes to change and the unannounced culvert.

All day that moment the horizon somersaulted perfectly beyond the windshield.
All day the extra quarter-turn so he could hang there in the white ditch singing
the origin of human beings.

THE INVENTION OF WATER

Their silence fills a mutual grief
older than themselves. They noticed such weather

in their parents, in the great models
that came before even them. Each passing

was a first death and a last. Everywhere
and always, when they discover the other

in the night, it's not a new body
they find but the oldest knowledge, whisper

at the neck, tongue in the ear. Reader, don't
compare their solitude with your own. Remember,

instead, what new thing came to you once,
old as your life on earth. Then go back from there

to the invention of water. Admit, if pressed,
your love of the world drowns ferociously

and with gratitude in that sea, that under
those early stars it concentrates itself

in the weight of a hand, the odd breath
of another finding you over

and over again in the dark.

THE BLUE HOUSES

They arrived at that place on separate evenings,
one of them balancing a bicycle on his nose, one knitting a sweater from lichen,
   one humming a song they all knew but could not name, one with her left
   hand on fire, one icing a motley-colored, five-tiered cake, one holding a tin
   cup overflowing with coins.

They made a city of themselves, continued in the art of their arrival but, after
   time, added one new thing. It wasn't long before
one of them juggled a small elk and salmon, a junco balanced on his nose, one
   braided a rope so strong it helped drag an ocean-going ship to safe harbor,
   one crowed barefoot every morning from the highest cedar shingles, one
   drew whole scenes in the air—mansions, elms, automobiles—before they
   vanished in minutes like fog, one went inside his hunger for a week before
   emerging with a burnt-orange glow, one made each of them a special coffee
   brewed slowly through the night so as to capture any unremembered dream.

On the last day, they all headed east,
one of them swallowing swords, carrying two local orphans on his back, one
   weaving a basket of cordgrass and salt, one with a song straining to lurch
   from a breast pocket and turn the sky a new color, one presenting stigmata
   where a hand had been aflame, one carrying the round loaf of bread, clothes
   hung from him like sails on an ancient mast, one with the sweet well water
   of this place, sloshing in the bowl of his palms, blessing the path, leaving the
   blessing behind.

They arrived at that place on separate evenings. They made a city of themselves.
   They all headed east because there was nothing left of west. Nostalgia would
   not infect them. This had not been a fable, an allegory, a symbolic drama, an
   arrangement of surrealistic tableaux. The well water had been sweet. And
   the company. And then, just as every day since, they stepped into the next
   suggestion. Not claiming anything. Not a thing.

THIS

What you wanted was bread on the table,
your shoelaces tied. An aisle seat. Passwords
that did not change. You wanted music
coming out one wall of your house, huge
music bent and curved as from a band shell
the shape of the Hollywood Bowl. You wanted
to bite the ear lobe. You wanted the body
at the end of the tongue no different than
language. You wanted my eyes and your
fingers shutting them when I died. We were
prisoners of hope then, under a hot
sun on the calmed ocean, barely steadied,
near falling from our small raft of belief.
What you wanted was epic, someone else
will say. You wanted awesomeness. But you
didn't, really. Not the *I'm about to*
die standing here in front of God   awesomeness
or the *I have lost control of all*
bodily functions and am pissing and
shitting down my pant leg awesomeness. You wanted
most of all to recognize the shimmer
of this desktop, and that cushioned arm chair,
and the light this afternoon the same color
as the fallen leaves across the boulevard,
and the auras, the *I swear to God* auras
people walk around inside all the time
down your sidewalk, only now you just noticed—
which is truly awesome, you think—that what you never
asked for in a million years makes you want it
now, forever, more than breath almost, more
than breath, almost. You want the haloes over
people walking back to their homes, over
their little dogs, and the squirrels whose excavations
bear responsibility for the ultimate

collapse of your yard. You want the squirrels
forgiven. The dirt forgiven. Its collapse
into the unknown basement of day. You want
everything holy again, someone will say.
But you don't, really. You want—there isn't
a word for it—this thing, this thing. And this.

THE VENICE BOARDWALK

Secret Father waits
until she's twenty to break
the news. Skateboarders

weave around them in a roil.
He'd been the one to buy her

coffee and a roll,
to talk long in the wave-churned
haze about common

friends or the architecture
of forgiving. She saw whole

desperate blocks flattened
to sand. He a tsunami
that might unhinge them

if they let it, all the grief
one grief beneath that blue noise.

BEFORE

1.

Smoke swims out
the cabin stove pipe, binding
to fog

the way a gray
overcoat joins the mob, swelling
toward the park,

the way maple
leaves fall, fanning the green
of the great lawn.

2.

I watched my father leave one Wednesday
bound in a truck for no good. Years later I saw
my mother open her eyes to the sick-bed

ceiling, close them to waves at Venice Beach,
the click skates made along the boardwalk, the icy
orange pulp the stranger brings her at a stand

before he offers a Pall Mall, before
he leads her, one north step after the next,
all the way to the Santa Monica pier.

3.

On the interstate ahead of the storm,
    slow pulses of light shine

into Oklahoma, Kansas, Missouri,
    great dark interiors

furnished like grandparents' parlors,
    places we escaped to

winter daytime, the china pattern
    a maze, faces on the wall

a kind of people we recognized, those
    we could never really know.

4.

In the mountains where
November ends, the lake turns,
bear over bear, before

ice races toward the middle
from each shore, before
char, rising and falling,

eat everything.

5.

If you ever have to bury men
alive, like I do, you'll know to spend

affection nimbly, prodigal, the last
coin the day all money turns to sand.

6.

Before my second son was born I wished,
first thing, as he was lifted up fresh
from his mother, to smell the ocean

of his head. I told nurses not to hurry him away
or wash whatever blood or mucus
still clung to him. I wanted to hover

close, in my own time, above the beating fontanel,
the small red hairs slicked by dark swimming.
In the middle of the continent, I wanted

to know the nearness of salt, to finger
that place on the neck where gills had been, where skin
now kept its secret as the head sagged

clumsily, the head of a giant turtle,
come to shore on the wave more powerful
than itself, suddenly on sand, the tide

having receded, the air new, that light
bright and new, every human being on the beach
rushing that way now to touch it.

OCEAN-GOING

—after an installation by Doris Salcedo

The green water, Lake Michigan, nags a jetty beside the grand public park, gives
    way to the blue water, Lake Michigan, the ocean-going freighter there in the
    far rain-haze at the end of color.
Long ago, the house I lived in, west Los Angeles, tethered itself to its hill, its cul-
    de-sac, a crescent of oleander at its edge.
It's hard to know the weight of rose petals sewn into a shroud for the
    disappeared. At the museum it fills a room the size of a chapel, sweeps like a
    weather system across a thumbnail of cruelty, a planet of sorrow.
I leave that place in search of a great body of water.
I left that first house baptized but not confirmed.
The artist carved niches in the white walls and in each placed a pair of shoes
    belonging to one of the unnamed. Covered the hole with transparent fabric,
    sealed it shut with thread of human hair belonging to one of the unnamed.
That house slid into a boulevard during the last rains. In Los Angeles, the rains
    find their way to the ocean through the usually dry concrete washes, where
    people whose houses are shopping carts live under oilskin tarps.

BLESSING

Finally he just needed pavement
under his feet and walking, three
jays on that wire, that cloud, that glint
off fascia on the old man's house.
He needed the man's wave through glass,
schnauzer in the next window, then
neighborhood thinning, giving way
to high rise, cab stand, independent
bank, pizza kitchen, saloon, store
after store just turning on lights
and wheeling signs on the walk.
He needed the furniture man,
the one who twenty years ago
shooed his son from a couch. He met
his eyes and blessed him. He blessed the
green bench under a hickory
tree circled by brick. He forgave
the post office, its little flag.
Finally he just needed pavement
because, as a man, he could not
sit still, even if a spirit
called, even if it said, Philip,
or George, or Hank, I need you to
sit quietly in the half light
of your living room and let your
water table drop to zero.
Let the bark canoe holding you
to eye level turn like the needle
of a compass, falling with you
toward the basement of your inner
dark. Everyone you have ever
hurt is waiting there. Each small thing
you have ever loved waits to hear
your miracle voice. Even if

that spirit called, he might have found
himself at this pond, two miles from
home, these geese squabbling, the semis
fluttering by. No one quite like him
has seen the ripple coming now
his way, wave like a little word
soon to be in his mouth. No one
quite knows the way he does how the word,
going in like forgiveness, will
come out like juice of these berries,
bite of this wind. He may not have
moved three inches in this life—still,
his hands full of zeroes, even he
knows enough to bless, to bless.

MEMORY OF WATER / WINTER SUN

—a painting by Brian Frink, 2015

I'd lived a long way away
from myself, nearly ready
for owl or wolf, song without song

the frozen creek might sing. Where
the blood begins, I don't care.
No need to know grief's origin

to allow for its laying on
of hands in the kitchen one
blue dawn. Coffee steams in the face

of the ten thousand things.

2. Disappearances

Why I come here: need for a bottom, something to refer to;
where all things visible and invisible commence to swarm.

—*C.D. Wright*

WATERSHED

My grandmother sent me to bed those days at last light, leaving the dark to adults on the cabin's front porch. The sound of the creek made me sleep, but not before I counted its dozen voices over stone and pictured gnats balled in their ellipses, like cartoon atoms, over the roil. My grandmother sat for the first time all day. My mother smoked. My grandfather struggled in a metal chair to read the last good stories in the *Los Angeles Times*. No one flipped on the outdoor bulb because of the moths it drew. The last horsefly pecked and buzzed at the screen.

The sound of the creek made them talk. Maybe, like me, they heard their own voices in the water. Maybe, like me, the water gave them words. All that conversation fed by snow from the eastern Sierra. In no time, even in that heat, the melt plumped alfalfa fields along the narrow road to Bishop. It filled the bellies of horses.

They talked about time. I thought a lot of the one black widow under the floorboards waiting that week to find me, but before I slept I mostly heard them talk about time. A Scottish city where his father was born. My grandmother's Idaho. My mother's life before children. *All gone*, they would sometimes say. Then they would start again.

I don't know how much of this is dream. The creek made me sleep. The porch filled with story and dark.

Then came the morning we drove back to LA, down the Owens Valley, its water stolen by the city, its lake turned to alkali flat, most farms gone bust. One desert edge, a sentry gate—all that was left of Manzanar. A dirt road, a sign pointing into the White Mountains—some brutal crest where bristlecone pines first began to live two thousand years before me.

As I grew into a young man, I was afraid of cities and of mountain passes. Both took my breath away. If I was driving, in eight lanes of freeway traffic or on a two-lane pass at 8,000 feet, my arms could turn to stone across the steering wheel. I was only learning then about panic attacks. It never occurred to me that the closeness of people, or the impossible distance from them, could produce the same result. I did not want to leave this life.

Sometimes I would not be able to make it stop—was not able to tell myself, as I can now, *Go ahead and die*. Words which became, after a while, a cure for my anxieties. The thing that makes me breathe again. *All gone*, the three of them would sometimes say. Then they would start again, the creek still falling its thousands of feet out of ice into the lives of animals.

LOOKING FOR THE MAN ONE MORNING TO DUSK

You find the man in the empty shoes of your grandfather's closet.
You find the man in a hand reaching from sky, jingling keys at the level of your
eyes.
You find him whistling as he waits for the light to change.
You find him in the calm rush of the ravine, smell of turpentine and sage, 7000
feet, the Eastern Sierra.
You find the man moving the tongue around in his mouth when he threads a
fishing hook, looping the line twice before the knot closes.
You find the man wrapping the Rainbow in a bed of willow leaves in your creel.
You find him in the afternoon nap, the unfinished chapter on his chest.
You find him singing to his wife after only one whisky.
He lets you make the next: a single ice cube, a splash of darkness from another
land.

AUGUST FIRES

The month before I was born, my stone
mother moved back to her parents' house,
walls to each side of her sliced thin as flakes
of skin, narrow as finch song pushed through

windows and doors to an ear. Who knew
brown liquors of smog lay all along
the coast, and waves pushed up the sand saying
her name once, again—each a lover,

and this stone mother too far away
to hear them, any sound not a choir
of dust. I was born to that quiet house,
the slate interior, the granite hum

and the rocking and the song that once
she could sing again moved out the screens,
across August hillside fires to the sea,
where a painted boat would wait, leaning.

RIVERSIDE, CALIFORNIA

The city was the father
who beat him to quiet. No

wonder the mysterious
flights to the desert, the dry

lake between his ribs bruising
into this one, that one, each

angry outburst of the moon.

AIRSTREAM

—a photograph by Julie Blackmon

The round meadow edges those woods
a canoe leans into as time begins
to end. From out of frame, a cloud
of poison drapes us for the bugs. The wind

will stop. It always stops, but not
for us. As in the city, wolves need room
to move before we find them out,
before inviting them to play. Our mom's

out walking. Our dad promised fish
for dinner. Trout, these wolves are all we wish
for, ever. By ourselves, in fear
of dark. Parents gone, no sweet song to spare.

KITCHEN IN LOS ANGELES

My right sleeve caught fire in 1961. My grandmother's flowered dress had turned
toward the breakfast nook wallpapered with hibiscus.

It must have been a favorite. I remember its length and cotton from photos and
from life. I wonder if her dress wanted to join the flowers behind the red-
leather curve of seats. She never saw me burn.

A tent of blue grew above my flannel arm, blue as the gas ring under the
saucepan of milk. Even now, the muscles remember jerking something
invisible to the floor, as if a spider had crawled across my hand and would
not fall. The hand and arm threw down again, again, until the flame went
out.

On days my grandmother hosted canasta, her friends sat beneath the wall of
Hawaiian flowers, dentures slipping if they laughed too hard, their little hills
of See's Bridge Mix eroding. Nothing in their lives blazed at that moment.
Their blue hair fluttered like the calm lights of the aged. Their crooked
fingers turned cards face-up on the tabletop without pain.

It wasn't their calling to tell me about trouble in Cuba, or the sad wilderness of
my mother, or the neighbor who threatened to kill us if we sold our house to
Blacks.

On those days, I stood by the range with the bread board pulled out, making
my peanut butter and mayonnaise sandwiches. Between deals, I pushed the
button on the electric shuffler. The women told me the names of their own
dear ones.

Soon enough, my new sister would be born, and the Baldwin Dam would break,
and Watts explode. I leaned against the range. I was too young to know what
human beings could do to each other. What angels like these sailed so close.
What hard dangerous things, machines that could turn everything to ash,
pressed at me from behind.

LOOKING FOR THE MAN IN A THIRD GRADE
CLASS PHOTO

No one ever knows who she looks at
finally, in such eternal moments,
Katsuko burning him through and still through
with her fabulous eyes. Nor Tragg Gunn,

poor spondee, a boy whose life grew, we
can all hope, more lyrical than his name.
No one should know what iron filing
finally lodges in the heart, or if

a comet delivered it, or a
dull music. He was, in his young way,
in love with the Japanese girl. He was,
in his own way, alarmed by ugliness

in two words. When a man is, atom
after doubling atom, the current
destination of such things, what can the
thirty-eight of us do but bore in

to the silver gelatin behind
the lens, inside the cave where an oracle,
who wants nothing to do with us now,
reads God's verdict to another age.

WE KISSED ON THE LIPS

We kissed on the lips. In the morning, still half-asleep, we kissed him on the lips at the breakfast table, his face turned up from the *Los Angeles Times*. In the evening, hovering above the couch, we kissed her on the lips before going to bed. We kissed on the lips to say goodbye in the evening, on the lips to say goodbye when we left for college, on the lips to say so long when we left for good.

We kissed on the lips saying hello to the aunt and uncle come to our house for Easter Day. We kissed Nana on the lips, even after she rubbed a wet diaper on her cheeks to tone her skin. We kissed Elsie on her British-speaking lips. We would kiss a new brother on the lips if we got one. We kissed our new sister on the lips when she surprised us in the middle of our lives. We kissed Curly the dog on the lips and Fitzhugh the dog on the lips. They kissed back.

We stopped kissing those few awkward years and shook hands through our teens. We hugged and we patted on the back. We put one arm across another shoulder and sometimes squeezed. When we became adults, we kissed sisters on the lips again. We kissed male and female cousins on the lips. We kissed friends on the lips. We kissed lovers on the lips to say we loved them. We kissed them on the lips to confess. We kissed to forgive. We kissed lovers on the lips in order to betray them.

After the stroke, we kissed our grandmother's lips, even as a thread of saliva moved down her chin. We kissed our grandmother on the lips, even as she struggled to sit up in the rented hospital bed under her own roof, trying to swallow. We kissed our brother-in-law with AIDS on the lips. We kissed our grandfather's lips, already sewn shut, that afternoon he lay in his coffin. We kissed our grandfather on the lips.

We kissed napkins and windows and, faraway in Paris, Oscar Wilde's grave. Once, when you were talking, we kissed you on the lips. It didn't slow you down at all. It made what you said more musical. There in the sidewalk café, you held the cup to its saucer. The traffic thickened along the boulevard, even as it grew silent. We kissed you on the lips, and music played at the edges of your mouth and at the doors of bars and night clubs. Still, it became a thing, finally, as rare as Eskimos and their noses, as rare now as ice and time.

INSIDE THE ANCIENT BOWL OF WATER

Before the downed fighter jet, 50 years
too deep until sonar could detect it,
before 100 years of glittering tackle

and leaded line, the summer furniture
no one could burn, shoes of the suicide,
the wedding ring, bottles and cans, a hammer,

a Dodge, that's when the water monster hovered
over the darkest bar of sand, waiting
for glaciers to stop melting, for first lines

of daylight to stoop to it, just as a boy
waits inside his dream of drowning for
the surface of the next day to find him.

MY FATHER WITHOUT ANSWER

In his last months, my father shuffles room
to room, and when he speaks his voice begins
and stays at some upper register lost

since he was a boy. Maybe it's the inner
ear, maybe the meds: He's back on the Navy
deck, 1946, not knowing where

one foot will land. He doesn't rave. He's not
helpless. But he won't know where the ship sails
until he gets there, the cane his only

weapon anymore: for pointing, to stand
up straight. In his last months, he never says
goodbye. If he tried, the sound of him would

only squeak anyway, sound the hinge made
that day our mother closed the door on him
for good. That morning, because it was his

job, because he had no other answer,
he drove his semi-load all those hours
to the secret test site in the desert.

LOOKING FOR THE MAN IN THE MOON LANDING

The man in the moon, I mean. I knew
the graven image at the end of wax,
each eye a sea. Month by month, the mouth
telling its grief sideways to inaudible

space, even as humans burned to ash
on their launch pad, circled
the home planet until forced back to air, serially
defeated, each capsule glowing

like a cigarette in descent. And then that
morning, everyone up at 5:00 AM, humans
racing to the moon's rescue with foldable ladder,
spade, and flag. Fifteen, I looked

for the being who might percolate
through dust to greet them, someone I could
become, feather-light, breakable,
speaking a universal tongue. How would

I know if the command module, rounding
the dark side, slung back to Earth, carried a moon man
with its load of rock? His foolishness or crime
forgiven. His banishment complete.

LOOKING FOR THE MAN ON THE SIDEWALK

The man under a garbage bag singing Lead Belly to his own breath.

The man in a gray checked suit.

The man like my grandfather, Los Angeles 1958, walking on thin leather with the pickets.

The man whose child grows from one hand, whose woman's arm loops through his.

The man stepping out of a cab, across rainwater to the democracy of stone.

The man who sings too loud or goes crazy too wide, building-side to curb.

The man looking up, like a hick from wheat country.

The man looking up, wondering at the strength of glass.

The man weeping into his collar.

The man who sings Enrico Caruso singing opera.

The man stopping to tear at a scab on his wrist.

The man who tells time with each step, telling a story each time looking at his watch, tearing at a scab.

The man fearing his own strength, the animal body, walking out of a bar into light.

The man afraid of his father's name.

The man who remembers the last day in the Army, folding and stowing.

The man thinking about his grandmother under a hot helmet in the beauty salon.

The man whose ears ring like tin.

The man who stares straight through everyone else's body.

Like standing up in a small boat halfway across the ocean.

Like standing up knowing there's something over that far curve.

MEMORY OF WATER / AFTERNOON IN MARSEILLES

—a painting by Brian Frink, 2014

Along the quay at the fish market,
a boy goes missing among

knots and water lines, the colored flags,
the tables of octopus

and bream. How could he know
when he let go of the hand he'd swim

through damaged net, through secret
adult song to an unannounced ledge,

place his mother's hand finds him
at last, where she scolds him in the great

red lines of day, this woman
he can never know again, this stranger.

THE MAN SAILING TO PATAGONIA

Above the ferry it rained
on each rusting hinge, ten lead

layers of paint, all across
the impossible knots. When

would he break again inside
the cabin. How brief each piece

before the gale would not know him.

ACROSS EL GOLFO DE PEÑAS

—southern Chile

Once in a man's life he must
go deep inside the heart of

complicated sea, past shredding
rocks, to where the mermaid

teaches him to breathe under
water, even as she makes

the rust, the iron wreck of him.

MEMORY OF WATER / CONSTELLATION NIGHT WATER

—a painting by Brian Frink, 2014

We found ourselves turned around after the storm,
entering harbors we knew only from

maps of the other world. These stars could not
help. We recognized this trough from a desert

all of us had crossed, a set of mountains
we'd all climbed. All that was lifetimes ago. We

survived on small fish the boy would pull up,
mackerel or sardine, scarred fish but whole.

Rain filled the pails daily with a new story.
Clouds, finally— After the clearing, clouds

saved us in their way, small rare bodies
just overhead between us and a blue

routine. They yielded. They yielded until
nothing remained and they were everywhere. The next

darkness came on, dragging its infinite
alphabet of light. Someone began to sing.

LOOKING FOR THE MAN IN THIS WOMAN

The woman in this photo who taught me my name.
The woman in that photo who pulled me up from the edge of the outdoor
    landing, hanging two stories above the stone.
The woman who reached into my chest and pulled out lungs and a heart.
Looking for the man in her, as in a mirror made of ways of talking or dressing,
    the ear she opened.
The woman I could be for her, although I will never know.
Looking for the man in the walking body I didn't know I wanted to become.
Looking for the man in this woman each time she showed me a new place to
    touch, that new thing to write on the chalkboard at the back of the skull.

LOVING A WOMAN

Understand the young man does not know he wants to fall and fall and fall until he cannot recognize himself any longer. The air rushes up from under him, each building a blur, even as one face, then another, snaps into focus at their windows. Gravity will have its way with him.

The young man does not know a lovely suicide comes first with its awkward quiet, every word a deserter, its one dull thud in the chest. Even if he knew the language, he might not use it.

For this reason, he can only talk with others about his face in her breasts, the nipples hardening, the size of his cock, the damage it could do. It's a story told by firelight, the owls and coyotes singing across the dark surface of night. It's a story that keeps the other beasts away. It puts the boy in him to sleep.

In this way, he will separate from his mother, even as he does not know he wants to fall back into her.

Still, sometimes in dream, all the gear ratios dissolve and his hands turn to water on the face of someone beside him. Then her body turns to rain. Then they fall from the sky inside the same storm. All through the day, the dream will make him tired.

For all of his life, days have moved forward or backward. Even now, the road unfolds from the horizon as he crosses the Mojave toward the next great city of light. The hard edge of curb and door stay the same. The palm trees survive their drought and the cars running into them. He never changes his name.

Still, the sky wheels above, and the ground manufactures holes for the innocent to fall into. Understand he will never suppose this. He prays to the god who is around the corner, waiting at the roadside café. He could never imagine a god who might wear the disguise of earth. He would never suppose that where the fault lines met he might find a door to the next world.

OLLANTAYTAMBO

If our name for sky did not
have God in it, what are we

doing, then, leaning into
embrace like sheaves of quinoa

in a small field, or laying
our bodies down like corn to

dry, such harvest, in the sun.

DISAPPEARANCES

—To remember is to pass through the heart of those who are absent.

Her boarding the train with such a small bag of things.

His stopping at the corner before turning to drive nearly all 700 miles west in the dark.

The salmon landed, their last silver dances on the boat deck.

The swallows and finches that have stitched our skies.

The look at your mouth, not seen for years now, even though we have rarely been apart.

The willow the creek bent around.

The Chinese elm, center mast of those last months in Los Angeles.

Silences of my grandfather meaning a new death had arrived, and the luck. Silences of my grandmother meaning the suffering of the body would stay, and the grace. Silences of my mother meaning shame that never left, new joy she never felt deserved.

The road through the desert, valley to valley, one dry sink to the next.

The park filled with old neighbors, the forest edge, the beach where everyone faced the wave line and the blue immensity beyond.

The condor at the bottom of the world.

My plaid sleeve on fire at the kitchen stove.

The cyclist gone still at the curb.

A Loch Leven on my line up the far reach of the gorge, past the last cabin, the silent cougar, past any other voice, past disappearance to the other side of now.

3. The Oratory of All Souls

When I come home I am going to learn fresco painting
and then, if Jacques Raverat's project holds good, we
are going to build a church, and the walls will have
on them all about Christ. If I do not do this on Earth, I
shall do it in Heaven.

—*Stanley Spencer*

THE ORATORY OF ALL SOULS

—Murals by Stanley Spencer, Sandham Memorial Chapel, 1927-32

1. A Convoy of Wounded Soldiers Arriving at Beaufort Hospital Gates

Rhododendrons camouflage the iron
until the last curve up macadam

where the gates swing in, take three men
to open onto stone the lunatics

still call home. New arrivals wave their
flags at us—No, it's trucks of broken

bodies in a story of white slings.

2. Scrubbing the Floor

Where one dark meets the next in the long
corridors under the earth, a man

tracks in soap the wingbeats of angels.
All across the red tiles, body splayed,

the failed flights circle after circle,
the trays of bread sailing over him

toward every compass point of the hungry.

3. Ablutions

We would iodine the rib wound, pat
dry the bathed back. We would polish brass

fixtures for art, for a weekend pass.
We would take the arms, akimbo, down

from each invisible cross. We would
have you lather your own hair like that

on a body you might love again.

4. Sorting and Moving Kit-Bags

In the washed-out grays of the courtyard
those who can still point point orderlies

toward their padlocked bags. The bed-cases
can wait. In such a heaven, even

waiting is the first exaltation,
that and the suffering, the everyday

labor of the able, their eyes cast down.

5. Kit Inspection

We lay the stage, the rough dimensions
of a grave, the canvas ground sheet first

before the blanket, brown as fair earth,
blossoms with a shaving brush and gloves,

our rolled socks, a rations tin, Book of
Common Prayer. No weapons anywhere,

some just now beginning the reckoning.

6. Sorting the Laundry

The heaped sheets flying, orderlies call
out the names the nurse writes down, the named

clouds flying. And towels sail like striped
trapezoids, like bright metallic cowls

on malthouse roofs. A thick jacket dives,
a crow, a crow diving at the red

spotted handkerchiefs of the insane.

7. Dug-Out (or Stand-To)

We would rehearse our resurrection
even as we laid out the leather

and our canteens. Overnight, something
fire-filled had lifted. The barbed wire turned

to weather and fell back. We hadn't
seen this coming in our ditch. All night,

no candle, inside our little deaths.

8. Filling Tea Urns

After the clanking of tin, the loose
talk, the narrative of injury

or remorse, comfort sets out in each
direction toward the afflicted—what

he trusts, at least, the far passage still
unexplored, the man at the counter,

housed among lunatics without name.

9. The Resurrection of the Soldiers

Some of us spend the fullness of day
rousing to silence, still half-dazed next

to other fallen. Some untangle
the wire they spent their last hours wrestling

to escape. A man returns road-stones
to the creek. Bandages unravel

like ribbons on the day side of death.
These men shaking hands: They're just as

startled climbing from the earth by peace
as by the bomb blasts that drove them there.

And the mules, the mules have lain with us
all these months, holy in death, holy

now in their rising. And the white cross
attached to us when time stopped came from

a country no one fought for, no one
needs to claim. Christ collects each to his

robe in its irrelevance, there and
in a cloud heap above the altar,

the place where this end meets the middle
of a story the walls might tell, north

to east to south, beginning again.

10. Reveille

Dozens of times since, under one net
of shame, the next of retribution,

we find ourselves in the thin minutes
of dawn, hear the tent-flap pushed aside

and news of the end of war. It's then
we recall turning out, shaved and square,

first sun casting shadows behind us.

11. Frostbite

They will arrive in angel disguise
to scrape the smitten feet and remove

buckets of night poison. They remake
the beds inside a riot of flowers

on the wall, alongside the undone
puzzle, a patient in calico

dreaming of grass on his family's farm.

12. Filling Water Bottles

What could we ever carry in brief
to the next field that matches the spring

rushing from marble block, the drunken
morning that will sanctify even

the mules. So curious, this floating.
The topis tilt back with each swallow

making aves made of dun and blue.

13. Tea in the Hospital Ward

Bread and jam. Body, blood. No reason
miracle gifts should not multiply

in the advance of days. Crisp tie. Plush
white collar. No reason the girl won't

write or the wrenched leg mend. She had sent
the picture, after all. He rehearsed

the part in his hair, the words he'd say.

14. Map Reading

Since we already fell, already
rose, it hardly matters what new harm

the major plans for us. These berries
would have us sleep like animals, keen

to summer heat. He points his swagger
south, toward a valley. But we long since

entered our own country without him.

15. Bedmaking

Some new day he'd memorize the float
of sheet above the mattress, the sink

to blue stripe, the hospital-corner
tuck, his own fevered routine, but now

his lover, father, Giotto's church
pass their time on his wall, his body

cocooned in a wing chair, without wing.

16. Firebelt

We made spills of the news of the world,
burned an evening ring around ourselves.

We turned the muzzles of our cannons
to tent poles supporting the wildest

knots and pulleys. At night, black on black,
we retired to an orbit of our

own making, crawled inside our own moons.

17. Washing Lockers

Where round meets angle, where burlap meets
grace, he kneels down, rechristens the wood

grain for the hundredth time since the tree.
Where every pipe in the asylum

comes to meet, he's deep between the red
tubs, side-by-side hearts, the place where stiff

brush and hands reclaim the soul's first dark.

18. Camp at Karasuli (North Wall)

And God commands the pig be slaughtered
and men this hillside morning break bread

with rashers of bacon to the great
glory of their task. The man gathering

roots will crack the earth no less
than soldiers birthing boulders, nagging

them to smaller stone for the Serres
military road. And the mules will

be fed, and the dog nosing empty
tins. The rendering continues, news

at knifepoint and the tidying hand.
Stone after stone makes its way east, half

toward the road, half toward the man without
eyes, mouth, each pouch held out like ransom.

19. Riverbed at Todorovo (South Wall)

And God commands the river rock be
gleaned even as a team picks at cliffs

in resurrected counties. Men play
bingo in the heat. One beats his clothes

clean. One mends a shoulder tear as sheaves
of wheat arrive by muleback, each long

gun long returned, base metal, to the
ground. Those olive trees heave with shade. Hell

will not exist here. Small stones will make
their way to where a man crouches, lays

to make the great mosaic, a red
cross seen from the air. What won't press back

to dirt to make his art, a man's quick
hand and art will cast back to the stream.

4. That Beach

But I also think that the only meaning of art, its only purpose...is to make life more humanly livable. In brief, we should keep on proposing Paradise, even if the evidence at hand might indicate such a pursuit is folly.

— *Raúl Zurita*

THE PAST COMPLETE

My father's father drank until blind. He
beat my father bad and often. Who knows
what drives a man to blacken the eye, break
a boy's arm? We want a diagnosis.

My father's mother gave him to the nuns
to save his life. Then took him back, surrendered
him again. She worked around the worst drunks
and took her beatings too. And don't dare

judge her for not leaving. Our comfort wants
the danger gone, boy and woman safe, the past
complete. But my father's father, even
now, could use the terrible love of our
imagination. To stop the hour.
That fist. To hold this through-line between us.

2551

Government diverts $10 million in hurricane relief to
immigration enforcement. (New York Times, 9.12.2018)

An island is a place difficult to help because it floats far away with water all
    around it.

A child is a person easy to lose because when she calls for her parents we have
    already sent them away.

If we take millions from the storm, how could the storm ruin one more palm or
    tin roof.

If we add millions to the cages, how could that help us find a mother faster.
    She makes lunch somewhere out of earshot. Our calls, even at the highest
    volume, slip through the spaces of a cage. Like any other parent, they just
    disappear.

How could anyone know how complicated an island is. When something is
    surrounded by water, it floats alone.

What child in a cage expects to kiss anyone else. They might have thought twice,
    your fathers, presenting themselves at the shimmering gate.

You are two thousand islands in your cage. The desert makes an ocean all around.
    Your mothers, we hear, make lunch as we speak. We have built new oceans
    around them. Still, your islands and theirs form a chain we now have to
    settle on a name for.

VANQUISHED

Before she left for college, her father showed her how simply an index finger
will pluck out an eye, how easily, in one downward stroke, the ear rips away
from the head.

Years later, her newborn lay across her chest, still greasy with foam. She smelled
the air above his beating fontanel only to discover the sea.

In her middle age, she could still never imagine the ferocity of self-protection. At
some point in the middle of a bludgeoning, the accordion crush of metal, she
would go inside, past carefully arranged furniture and down a staircase to the
small dark room where she would wait to die.

Even now she recognized the tide that would overwhelm her son's attacker. How
through her hand it would snap the neck, close off the breath.

She will never confess that suicide, that murder.

Her garden slopes toward the river and its dream of endless motion.

All day long, in the middle of the country, she dreams of a beach scattered with
eavesdropping shells, and every few yards those clumps of kelp like hairlines
of the vanquished.

RESISTANCE

Since you took half the words away
the hill behind my house lost pine
and siskin, the sky some part
of its deep. Only yesterday
I walked the main street home, each tune
the grocer whistled a start

before it ended, store shutters
drawing, doors ajar—no one knew
who closed or opened. The word
escaping me was color. Town
gardens rioted in half-hues.
That was where the maimed or dead,

or what we used to call them, lay.
I still wonder where their names will go.
Inside my house, the half-things
still cling to their rooms, even though
a hill inside me makes a cave
for each key, book, magic spell:

hole in the earth that makes a mouth,
mouth in the ground that works to destroy you.

RIGOR Y AFECTO

—Valle de Maipú, Chile

In white chalk on the hillside,
inside a border of white—

the name of a wine, a brand
of paint, the way to sell cars,

or the last exhortation
high above the workers by

the dictator and his flies.

AMERICAN STORY

It would be so Brooklyn of you to tell me you lived in Brooklyn.

After a record thaw, the mountainside slid down onto the town of Thistle, Utah, in 1983.

When we rode our bikes in the national forest, we dreamed of outracing the mad chase of bears. Our bells jangled against the quiet. Can the young ever be forgiven? We were so naïve.

In Des Moines, a man stopped in the middle of his own bank robbery to weep over the terrazzo tile. *I'm sorry*, he said. *This is a turning point in my life. I don't want to miss it.*

You may think I'm toying with you. May wonder why, in this tiny car, I am driving to the Gulf of Mexico, to the recently rebuilt marina. And now to Wichita, where we await the vortex. Now to the scorched ground of Montecito, where the tiny car of words will sink wheels-deep into the ash.

It would be so Los Angeles of me to tell you I was born there. That I ate at places you have only read about in a James Ellroy novel. Like C.C. Brown's. Like Vince & Paul's. I saw the Baldwin Dam break open on live TV. I saw Gary Powers' helicopter go down. I saw snow on Huntington Beach. I lived in Los Angeles so long they named an earthquake after me.

Tell me your real name. My pink on your olive hand. My green eyes into your brown. We can begin again if we like. It's our birthright, the first American story.

HOW TO BE EVIL

Sometimes you just need to be yourself.
A sparrow falls, God won't lift a finger,
and neither need you, standing somewhere
nearby, smoking a menthol packed full
of winter sky, Caribbean sea, cool
beyond belief. When I kicked that sleeping
derelict in the head, I heard the gears
inside discover new torque. In my
suit and tie, I rode up and down the spines
of buildings making my deal, hearing
everyone's heartbeat loud as a fire I could
put out. Once I knew the way to reach through
a man, to wring his liver out
like a kitchen towel, beauty became
the plaything of violence, a daffodil
in its thin vase of acid, a two-year-old
walking the thin stone wall above the lake.
Sometimes I think I am the wind
ready to gust for a moment, long enough,
there at the parapet, to turn
a mother's distraction to regret. Sometimes
I am the water and the tide reaching up
to take his body in.

What do I have to teach anyone, after all?
God makes the weather. Persons weaker than you
control, for their small moment, huge
machines they are no match for. One is named
the body. One is named this room. You
at those tables drink from the same glass. Even
as you look this way, the woman in the next chair
has found her knife, the man his rough fist.
Beneath your small talk, the violence
already advances. Remember that blunt

87

word she let out five minutes ago? Remember
what he said last night, feigning
tenderness, about the faint pulse he saw
beating at your throat? When I leave
this spot, understand how large those things have grown
between you. Look at each other: Try to
remember when you didn't hate
that squint her eyes make when she says
your name. Try to remember when
you didn't hate his stupid hobbies, that childish
jaw line, that mouth, the road
to his lungs that even now seem ripe
for capture.

EXTRA

When loud music or the nakedness
does not break him, set the tape going

in the next cell. Each scuffle and thud
convinces, chair leg screeching across

the floor. Each final scream, each gun shot.

Wrap your partner's head in bloodied gauze
and lay him on a cart. Let the man

see guards cut the IV, small tremor
under blankets as he's wheeled away.

In the morning, be friendly. Offer
matches, a cigarette rolled from dung.

He will or will not get the message.
These gifts flare in the face, even burn

a little. Harmlessly. Harmlessly.

THE BOTTOM OF THE WELL

Even there you heard the reassuring voice, angel or ancestor, reminding you
about the light of day.

Even there, where stones wept their groundwater in the dark, you could stoop
to touch the distant ranges of your body. You could rise. You could make
yourself the long antenna receiving the first message from a star.

At different times your posture matched the curl of the hospice patient, the man
at the intersection kicked by rioters, the sprinter at the chalk, the woman
checking her tire along the county road, the boiler inspector, the man who
has convinced his son he is a camel and invites him to his back, the gardener
weeding.

Months before, something fell away or burned, and there you found yourself.
Something on the surface lifted. A cloth. A fog. The garment an action had
put on even before the action occurred or did not occur.

Something fell away or burned, and there you found yourself on the sidewalk
breathing the same air as pure motive. You were its hand now. You worked
for that small corporation.

The angel spoke plainly in your ear. *Eat*, it said, when food lay in reach. *Speak*, it
said, *even if it's dark and no one's listening.*

The ancestor pointed to the dime of sky. *Others have prepared the ceremony of
your return. You are walking there even now.* Just telling you about it, that
daylight blinds them.

APRIL

In the slow haul out of winter, his hand will remember how the wind kisses,
    finger by finger, the weakening arguments of the cynic.
A mile into woods, they found the missing boy, his tricycle dragging behind him.
    He ate the sandwich they gave him. He said he wasn't cold.
One day a woman could walk this neighborhood of old homes and not look back
    at every sound the melt or a screeching door will make. There in front of her,
    the finches, the wet street.
One day the woman will believe in the inviolable. The uncontaminated sun
    and moon have shone on her all her life. Unbroken history has colored her
    breath, her appetite. One day the body will accept its own destruction, one
    aching joint, one ischemic attack at a time, on its way to a perfect marriage
    with what made it.
Main Street prepares for its parade by sweeping walks and posting sales, by
    hanging the fluttering banners from one window to the next: *Welcome
    Home. Crazy Days.* The sidewalk fills with white shirts, the aroma of sugar.
In the slow haul out of winter, a hand will remember the name and plant it in
    the ground. In that way the ground enters the man. Through her eye across
    the blue, these finches. Through the boy's refusal, the boy. Everywhere the
    world turns back toward human beings as if, once forgotten, they'd grown
    new again.
And behind the slow-moving horses, behind the high school band glaring at
    noon, the gray dissidents are still marching: *Save Us.*

MOMENTS BEFORE

Everywhere and always, he sits on the tourist ledge
above Black Canyon, Hoover Dam a grinning idiot beneath him.

Always the undertow after a Mexican storm, his waving
to shore, the older girl stroking his way without effort to save him.

Everywhere the meadowlark's flute, the hum
in the desert middle, the question spilling in each direction.

And the road everywhere of her body, and always the place and the two
of them covered in dark, a temple built of silence.

The car in the first moments of its roll, always, the film of the world
tilting, and everywhere the windshield cracks.

What becomes forever of the neighbor on the fire escape, summer,
talking about Dostoyevsky. What of the line between there and the knife that
    stabs her.

Anyone forgets companions of concrete and storm. What of the Stellar's jay, the
    highway, everywhere
the woman never lover who lays down her life for you anyway, dies always
    rescuing your eyes.

MEMORY OF WATER / CONSTELLATION

—a painting by Brian Frink, 2014

The death of a star trails its light
all these billions of years

only to find a human drawing lines
pulse-to-pulse to build beast or archer.

We would make a story to see through the night.
Each stringed thing would wait for

extinction to find it, to undress
mythology and belief. In no time, not a thing

would remain but Leviathan
commanding the great curved deep, and above it

the face of the waters
and across that the first breath moving again.

THE REGIONALIST

The place you wrote about was you,
the white house, the grandparents who might
or might not whip you to poems come
evening, and the land unfolding here
and there, awaiting its stray bombs, Sunday
or any day, and the river running on
trout-jammed from snowpack to salt, a
ribbon of grace, Indian voices, a whim.

Geography and faith: Isn't
that what your effort amounted to, say this
storm without forecast, say this damage report, your
lean into event as if weather composed a life,
rain a wave breaking on that
far Oregon coast? You were a priest of the lost ancient
rite: You said the thing. The thing planted its kiss.

In the end, a ghost town is
what saved you. The slender
waiter pouring coffee in daylight and
cheer. Not the fallen roof. Not the crows. Her
hand patting yours with affection. The red
still in the sky. Not slag and rust. The hair
brushing against you making lights
among lights. The town was you, the
first voice of it, place to leave, a last gray wall.

AT LOW TIDE

All five of them made a point on the misshapen star a guided missile could find if
it cared to.

Back home in their towns, a rough ceramic bowl sat next to a vase of new
flowers. This was where one by one they would restore the light.

In the melody of this place, the creaking spruce trunk, brush or tap of crowns.
Labored bear breath. Whistling plover. Midnight glide of elk through the
scrub. Roar of a family on the ocean side of things inside the larger wave-
roar, waiting for the last faint push of foam to reach them. This heartbeat
at finger-end or in the ear. Rest when the wind stops to turn around. The
musical rest.

She stooped on the tidal flat a half-mile out at low tide, digging clams she would
not eat later.

A rocket across Gaza. Arc of weather ocean-to-bay. A helicopter gunship. A steel-
colored heron.

He hosed away eelgrass and mud before shucking the oyster, swallowing the
insides whole. Before that, he'd registered shape and texture, brine-scent and
color. It was like the way some honor the deer they have killed. It was like
corn meal on the ground for the spirit to pick up for its journey.

And what was there left to do but leave through the gates from before. Into the
mouth of new comfort. Into roils of tenderness. Into the vacancies of light.
Or the light of scar and bloody paving stones. The altar of the street. The
fragrance of lamb and coffee. Adhan wrung-out and being written on the air.

THE GREAT LITANY

For Lent, we twenty or so will begin with call and response: Four short lines of
　　praise for Creator, Redeemer, and Sanctifier. Forty long lines of petition.

To deliver us from our offenses and temptation. To spare others from their prison
　　cells, earthquakes, murder. To keep our President faithful to the oath. To
　　support workers in the field, open others' ears to good words. To forgive our
　　enemies, persecutors, and slanderers. To turn their hearts. Page by page.

We can barely stand for the whole prayer, some of us, the west window still dark
　　this time of morning, the baseboards ticking slow to temperature. The ocean
　　falls into itself two blocks away. We might stay upright if we could walk
　　there.

Our children all left us in their time. I know that much about these strangers.
　　One man has a tremor in his left hand. (Later, his wife will pass the plate for
　　both of them.) Another man, tall and bald, three pews ahead, wears thumb-
　　sized tufts of gray hair he missed behind one ear. (Later, he announces the
　　community dinner for immigrant relief. He is selling tickets.) You can only
　　see so much from this angle.

Our children all left us in their time. I know that much about these strangers.
　　Some had to change the locks. Some had to burn their own houses down. I
　　know they still wonder about it. They were workers in a field. It was harvest.

The ocean falls into itself two blocks away. Years back, bits of Fukushima
　　lingered there at first light, pushed up, pulled back in the foam. Early walkers
　　couldn't read the kanji. One dog ran to sniff, then shot back when the last
　　push of wave lifted the bits to its mouth. This is the Body of Christ, broken
　　for you.

We might stay upright if we could walk there. The nave filling with the heaps
　　of our requests: For all animals and fish in the sea. For our dead ones. For
　　travelers. For women in childbirth. For those suffering in mind and body.
　　The birds of the air. The clouds that will bring rain. For those blind of heart,
　　from pride or envy. For the end of war. For the end of loneliness. We could
　　walk there in any weather, reach our fingers down in the wash and bring the
　　salt taste to our lips. The Cup of Salvation.

SAN CRISTÓBAL HILL

—Santiago

For the Immaculate Virgin, they leave a picture of the son she saved from a mystery fever. Infant of the daughter they thought lost to gangs, daughter steered home by the daily candle. Grandmother made comfortable, even as her mind evades her. Grandfather lifting a suitcase to his side.

For the Mother of All, they leave barrettes, necklaces, thin leather wrist bands, holy cards, one plastic rose, an unfolded fan, red pencil, scapular of the beloved.

They leave a white ribbon, pink band that used to hold her hair in place, finger puppet, handkerchief tied in a bow, pacifier, shoe lace, sun visor the baby wore that day in the stroller.

They leave a child's rosary. And a child's rosary. And a child's rosary.

At the base of the statue of the Mother of all Mercies, no one knows which objects arrive here by grief, and which by gratitude.

A scapular needs to be worn to grant its promise: Where is the body it belongs to? The mother kissing her daughter: Is this before the surgery, or the last photo before the surgery failed?

No one is telling, here below the left ankle of the Immaculate Virgin, in a hollow below her base, where any whisper will not escape, even to the rains now dousing the candles, rains that move east to become infinite snow along the infinite granite rope of the Cordillera.

THE CAPTURE HAND

Sweeping the black king from the board.
On a shirt collar catching up, pulling a boy to the ground, where the bully begins
    to kick.
Holding the net, landing the brown trout.
Steady, and just one finger pressing to finish the photograph.
Clicking tight one pair of cuffs after another.
Signing the executive order. Pointing the pilot to where the despot sleeps.
At the end of a grandmother's arm, lifting him up and over the railing, where
    he'd hung five minutes before beginning to yell.
In the turbid water feeling in the dark eddy for another—O any part of the body.
On the buffalo robe like a bear paw counting coup, recovering the stolen pipe.
Receiving the host, the broken bread, the wine cup, the salt, the fish, the lamb,
    the thin broth—each prisoner of hope in her fashion.
Cupping fresh water streaming from the rock. Capturing first the lips, then the
    whole face.
In that economy, releasing and releasing again. Surrendering each thing.
    Breaking every chain.

AT THE MUSEUM OF THE DISAPPEARED

—Santiago

So we descend to the coup
like a beach at low tide, stone

by stone by broken bone. The
pools fill with urchins, each clam

its own page of history.
Then a voice commands us to

rise. It's the ocean talking.

MEMORY OF WATER / SHORELINE

—a painting by Brian Frink, 2014

Who knew memory
is concave. Who knew its tide
didn't need us or

our tiny boat. Just to wash
through and under it toward that

beach, that beach.

NOTES

1. The Blue Houses

The Theodore Roethke quote at the beginning of the section comes from "Meditation at Oyster River," part of The North American Sequence in *The Far Field*.

"At Spiral Jetty": *Spiral Jetty* is an earthwork by Robert Smithson at the edge of the Great Salt Lake.

2. Disappearances

The C.D. Wright quote at the beginning of the section comes from "Lake Return," one of The Ozark Odes in *String Light*.

"Disappearances": The quotation is from an audio guide to the Museum of Memory and Human Rights, Santiago, Chile. The institution is also referred to informally as the Museum of the Disappeared.

3. The Oratory of All Souls

The Stanley Spencer quote at the beginning of the section comes from a letter to his sister Florence and is found, among other places, in *Stanley Spencer*, edited by Timothy Hyman and Patrick Wright. The passage reflects an early dream of the artist, fueled by his admiration for Giotto, before being presented with the opportunity to create his murals at the Sandham Memorial Chapel in Burghclere. The masterwork's nineteen panels respond to the artist's World War I service in Bristol and Salonika.

4. That Beach

The Raúl Zurita quote at the beginning of the section comes from the introductory note to *Anteparadise*, translated by Jack Schmitt.

"The Regionalist": For Richard Hugo.

"The Great Litany": The long intercessory prayer of penitence and request is often incorporated into Episcopal services during Lent.

ACKNOWLEDGMENTS

Some of the poems in this book appeared first, a few in different versions, in the following publications. Many thanks to the editors for their belief.

Bennington Review: "My Father Without Answer"
Brevity: "Watershed"
Bridge Eight: "Begin," "Looking for the Man in a Third Grade Photo"
Burnt District: "The County Park in Fall," "The Venice Boardwalk"
Cincinnati Review: "Secret Father, Beginnings," "Secret Father Rollover"
Cloudbank: "American Story," "Memory of Water / Island," "Memory of Water / Winter Sun"
Field: Contemporary Poetry and Poetics: "Extra" (published as "For Extra Credit"), "Documentary"
Freshwater Review: "My Father Does Not Reveal Himself"
Hotel Amerika: "This"
Hubbub: "Inside the Ancient Bowl of Water"
I-70 Review: "The Man Sailing to Patagonia"
Image: "At the Shore"
Los Angeles Review: "Memory of Water / Shoreline"
Miramar: "Surfacing"
Nimrod International Journal: "The Oratory of All Souls"
Pebble Lake Review: "How To Be Evil"
Poetry Northwest: "Memory of Water / Constellation Night Water"
Salt: "Looking for the Man in the Moon Landing," "Disappearances," "Wave," "We Kissed on the Lips"
Saranac Review: "Looking for the Man in a Driveway"
Stand: "Resistance," "Loving a Woman"
The Blueroad Reader: Stardust and Fate: "Blessing"
The Southern Review: "Memory of Water / Constellation"
The Meadow: "Before"
The Wax Paper: "April"
Water~Stone Review: "The Bottom of the Well"
Weber: The Contemporary West: "Someone Else's Map," "Leadbetter Point," "The Invention of Water," "At Low Tide," "The Great Litany"

"2551" first appeared in *Michigan Quarterly Review*.

"Looking for the Man in the Moon Landing" was designed and issued as a limited-edition broadside by Bradley Coulter.

Many thanks to the following organizations, which offered space, time, or financial support that helped me make these poems:

> The Anderson Center at Tower View
> Hawthornden Castle International Retreat for Writers
> Minnesota State Arts Board
> Minnesota State Mankato Faculty Research and Faculty Improvement
>   Grant committees
> Prairie Lakes Regional Arts Council
> The Stanley Spencer Gallery
> Willapa Bay AiR

Thanks to my teachers, especially Allan Anderson, Rick DeMarinis, Glover Davis, Carolyn Forché, Madeline DeFrees, and Richard Hugo.

Thanks to my students for their fearlessness.

Thanks to poets Christopher Buckley, Ralph Burns, Patricia Clark, Jenny Yang Cropp, Luke Daly, Jordan Deveraux, Dylan Loring, Kate MacLam, Matthew Mauch, Thomas Mitchell, Andrew Nye, Lorna Pecard, Lex Runciman, Samantha Ten Eyck, Richard Terrill, and Michael Torres, who helped me make this a better book.

Thanks to Brian Frink, for his paintings and drawings and for our friendship, the gift of conversations about how to make art work. See www.brianfrink.com.

For Candace, always.

"Richard Robbins is a fiscal year 2021 recipient of a Creative Support for Individuals grant from the Minnesota State Arts Board. This activity is made possible by the voters of Minnesota through a grant from the Minnesota State Arts Board, thanks to a legislative appropriation from the arts and cultural heritage fund."

"This activity was made possible by an Artist Grant from the Prairie Lakes Regional Arts Council with funds provided by the McKnight Foundation."

ABOUT RICHARD ROBBINS

Richard Robbins was raised in California and Montana, taught in Minnesota for many years, and recently moved back west to Oregon. Before the current collection, Lynx House Press published his sixth book of poems, *Body Turn to Rain: New & Selected Poems*. Robbins has received awards or residencies from the National Endowment for the Arts, the Poetry Society of America, the Anderson Center, Willapa Bay AiR, and the Hawthornden Castle International Retreat for Writers. From 1986 to 2014, he directed the Good Thunder Reading Series at Minnesota State Mankato, which the Minnesota Humanities Commission called, "the premier small-town reading series in the country."